Times Tables Age 5-7

Melissa Blackwood, Liz Dawson & Stephen Monaghan

In a strange place, not too far from here, lives a scare of monsters.

A 'scare' is what some people call a group of monsters, but these monsters are really very friendly once you get to know them.

They are a curious bunch – they look very unusual, but they are quite like you and me, and they love learning new things and having fun.

In this book you will go on a learning journey with the monsters and you are sure to have lots of fun along the way.

Do not forget to visit our website to find out more about all the monsters and to send us photos of you in your monster mask or the monsters that you draw and make!

Contents

Grouping in 2s

Kora is sorting out the monster socks and shoes.
She has got into a monster muddle!
She has grouped these socks and shoes into **pairs**.

This can also be called **grouping in 2s**.

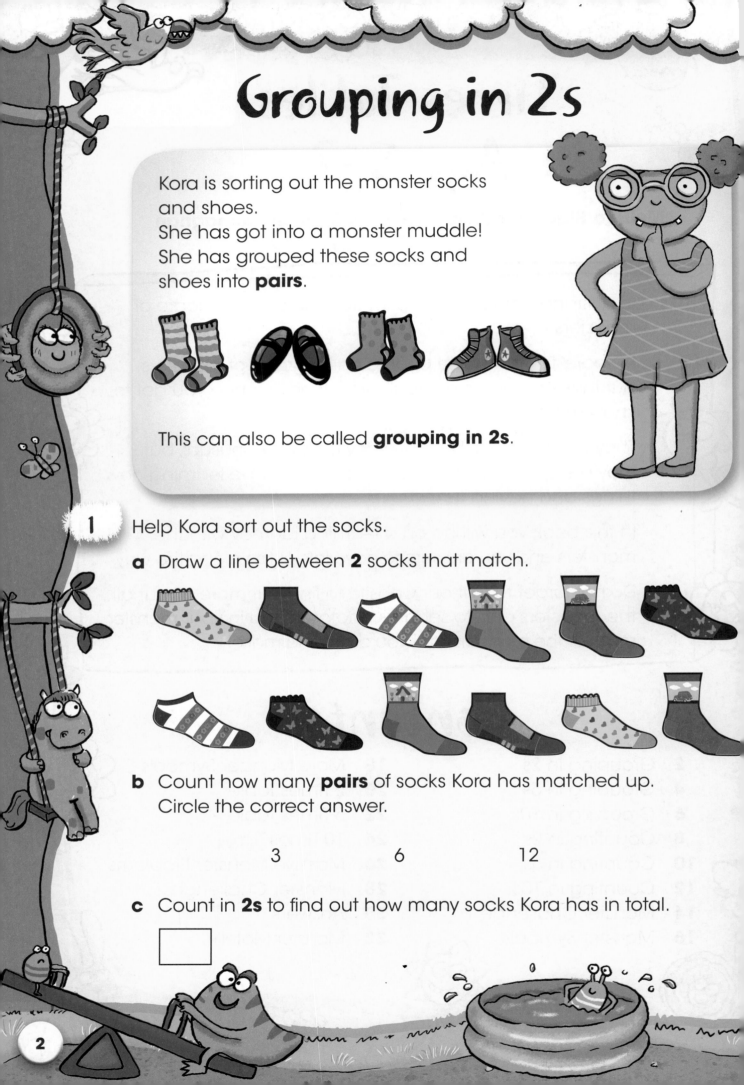

1 Help Kora sort out the socks.

a Draw a line between **2** socks that match.

b Count how many **pairs** of socks Kora has matched up. Circle the correct answer.

3   6   12

c Count in **2s** to find out how many socks Kora has in total.

2 The monsters are going to the mucky, muddy playground and need to wear their boots.

a Draw a **pair** of boots under each monster's name label.

(Poggo) (Nano) (Fizz) (Tizz) (Mum)

(Grandpa) (The Professor) (Gran) (Dad)

b Count in **2s** to find out how many boots all the monsters are wearing in total.

☐

c Complete the following sentence.

☐ monsters are wearing ☐ boots in total.

Fun Zone!

Make a monster sock puppet.

Monsterific! You can now find and colour **Shape 1** on the Monster Match page!

Monster Sock Puppet

You will need a sock, buttons for eyes, felt scraps or coloured paper for a nose, wool for whiskers, glue and scissors.

Ask an adult to help when needed.

1 Stick buttons onto the sock for the eyes.
2 Cut a nose shape from the coloured paper and glue this on to the sock.
3 Cut 6 strips of wool and glue 3 on each side for the whiskers.
4 Use the felt to give your monster spots or stripes.
5 Put your finished puppet on your hand!
6 If your monster sock puppet needs a friend, make another one. (Remember: that is a **pair**!)

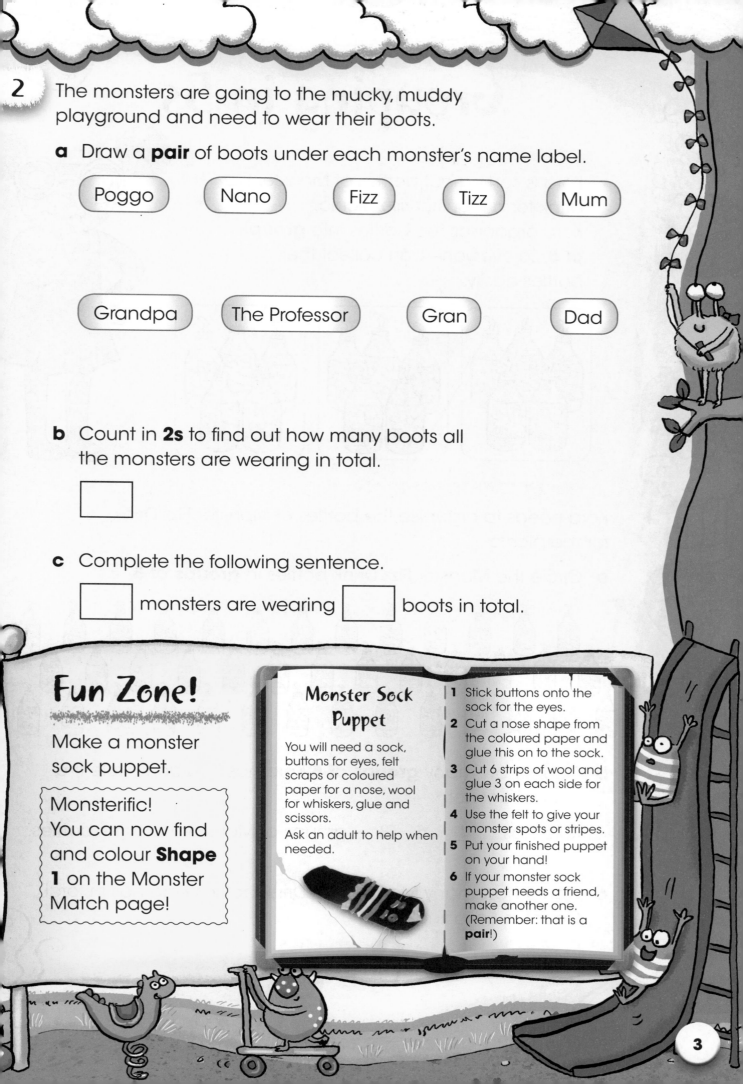

Grouping in 5s

Kora is sorting out bottles of Monster Fizz Drink for a Monsterville picnic.
Kora organises the bottles into **groups of 5**, so everyone can collect their bottles easily.

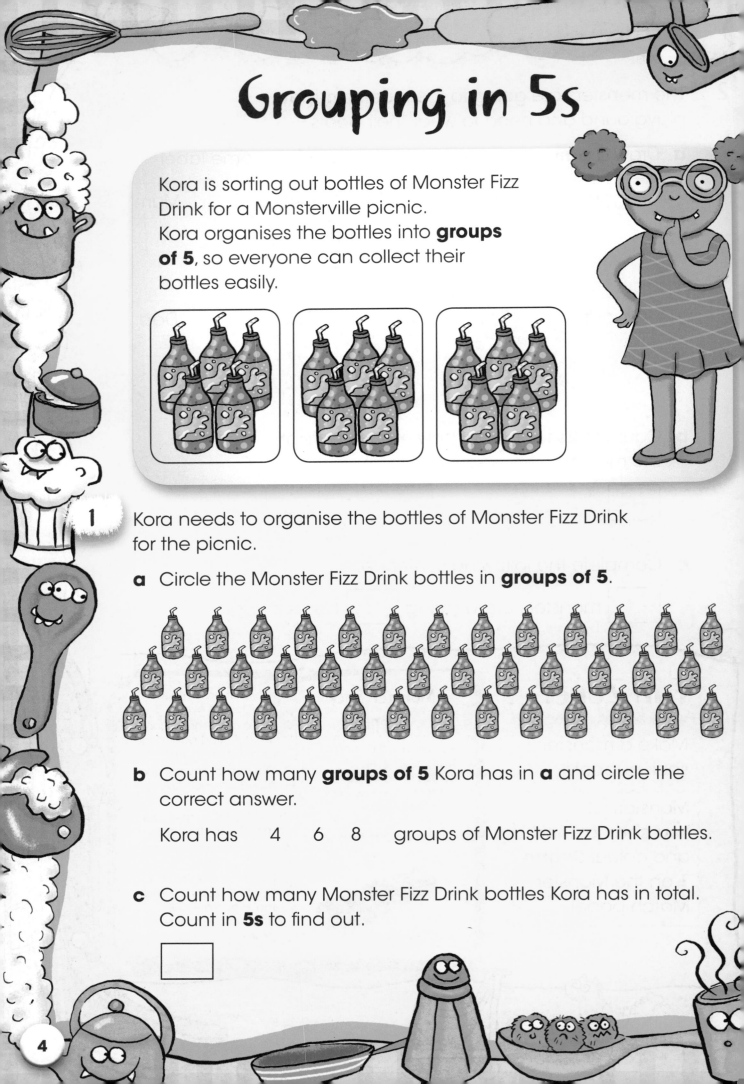

1 Kora needs to organise the bottles of Monster Fizz Drink for the picnic.

a Circle the Monster Fizz Drink bottles in **groups of 5**.

b Count how many **groups of 5** Kora has in **a** and circle the correct answer.

Kora has   4   6   8   groups of Monster Fizz Drink bottles.

c Count how many Monster Fizz Drink bottles Kora has in total. Count in **5s** to find out.

2 After the Monsterville picnic, Kora found 10 lost gloves.

a Count in **5s** to find out how many fingers there are in total. The first two have been done for you.

| 5 | 10 | | | |

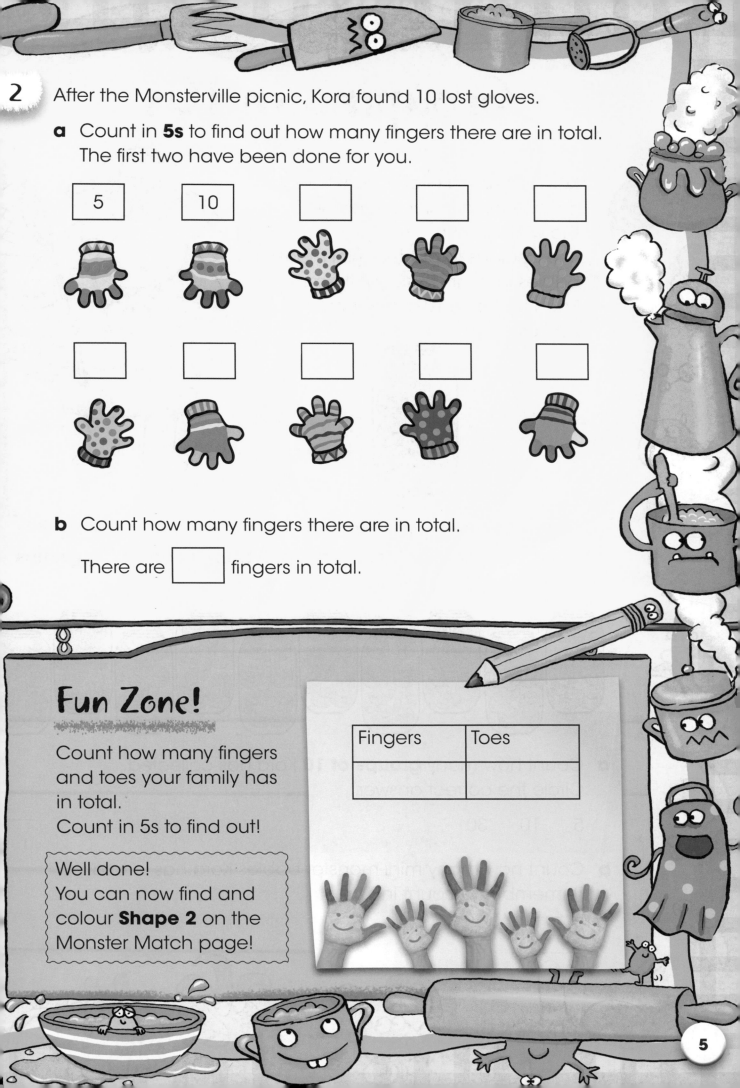

b Count how many fingers there are in total.

There are [ ] fingers in total.

Fun Zone!

Count how many fingers and toes your family has in total.
Count in 5s to find out!

Fingers	Toes

Well done!
You can now find and colour **Shape 2** on the Monster Match page!

Grouping in 10s

Kora is helping Gran count how many mini-monster babies live in the wild wood.
She decides to put the mini-monster babies into jars to count them.
Each jar holds 10 mini-monster babies.

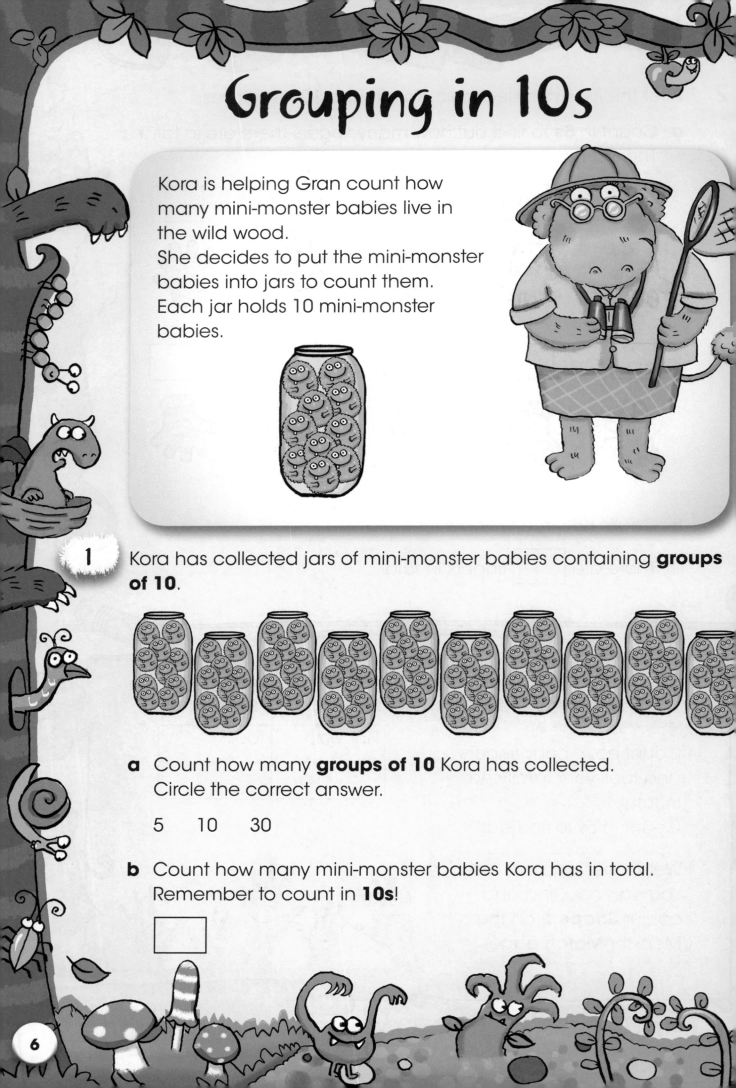

1 Kora has collected jars of mini-monster babies containing **groups of 10**.

a Count how many **groups of 10** Kora has collected.
Circle the correct answer.

5   10   30

b Count how many mini-monster babies Kora has in total.
Remember to count in **10s**!

2 Some of the mini-monster babies have escaped from their jars!

a Help Kora by grouping them back into **10s**.
Circle groups of 10 mini-monsters.

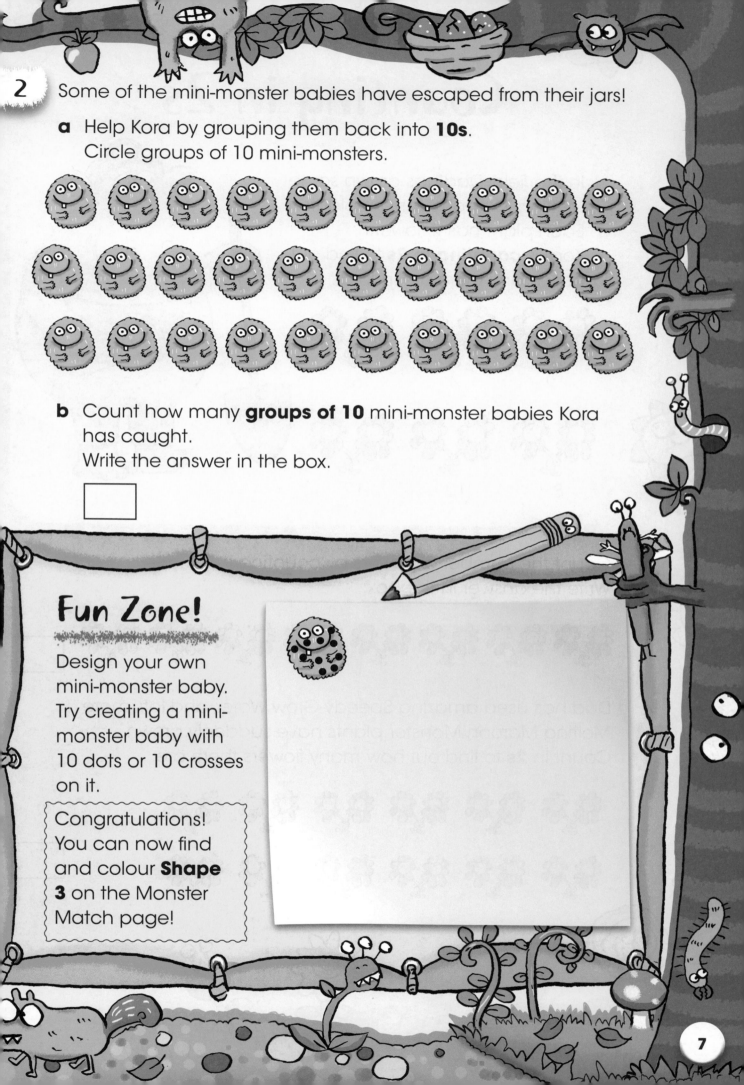

b Count how many **groups of 10** mini-monster babies Kora
has caught.
Write the answer in the box.

Fun Zone!

Design your own
mini-monster baby.
Try creating a mini-
monster baby with
10 dots or 10 crosses
on it.

Congratulations!
You can now find
and colour **Shape
3** on the Monster
Match page!

Counting in 2s

In the field, Dad has grown some Melting Maroon Monster plants. Each plant has 2 flowers. Kora is **counting in 2s** to find out how many there are in total.

2   4   6

8   10   12

1 Count the number of flowers by counting in **2s**. Write the answer in the box.

2 Dad has used amazing Speedy-Grow Water, and lots more Melting Maroon Monster plants have suddenly grown. Count in **2s** to find out how many flowers there are.

3 Webber is very impressed with Dad's flowers, and would like 20 flowers to decorate his home. Dad needs to work out how many he needs to cut.

Count 20 flowers and circle how many plants are needed. Write the number of plants needed in the box.

Fun Zone!

Make your own monster cress heads!

Well done! You can now find and colour **Shape 4** on the Monster Match page!

Monster Cress Heads

You will need eggs, cress seeds, cotton wool, paint and water.

Ask an adult to help when needed.

1 Cut the top off an egg, remove the egg inside and rinse the shell.
2 Paint the egg shell and leave to dry.
3 Paint some eyes and a mouth onto the shell to make a monster face.
4 Fill the shell with some damp cotton wool and sprinkle it with cress seeds.
5 Make sure it does not dry out and watch your cress grow over the next week!

Counting in 5s

Mum has been looking after Kora and they have been painting together.

On the way to wash their hands, Kora puts her fingerprints all over the walls in the living room!

Kora **counts in 5s** to see how many fingerprints she has made on the walls in total.

5 10 15

1 Write the number of fingerprints below each handprint, adding the extra fingers each time.
The first two have been done for you.

| 5 | 10 | | | |

2 Kora has accidentally put her fingerprints all over the kitchen too!
Write the number below each handprint.
Start at 25 and count in **5s**.

| 25 | | | | |

3 Help Kora find her way to the cloth to clean up her mess.
She can only travel by counting up in **5s**.
Start at 0 and end at 50.
Colour the squares to connect the numbers to make her pathway.

0	8	12	34	18	4
5	10	47	21	28	73
13	15	20	25	43	34
48	52	37	30	35	22
33	87	1	57	40	9
67	41	16	38	45	50

Fun Zone!

Have fun with handprinting.

Monsterific!
You can now find and colour **Shape 5** on the Monster Match page!

Handprinting

You will need coloured paint, paintbrushes and paper.
Ask an adult to help when needed.

1 Cover your hand with paint.
2 Press it onto the paper and leave it to dry.
3 Turn your handprint into a monster pet, using different colours of paint for eyes, whiskers, nose and mouth.
4 You could try printing a pair of hands to make a monster insect!

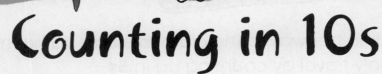

Otto has broken down!
He needs Kora to find the jars of bolts in his workshop.
Each cog in Otto's body suit needs 10 bolts to fix it.

1 cog needs 10 bolts.

1 Each jar has 10 bolts inside.
Circle the jars of bolts in the picture.

2 Check that Kora has enough bolts to fix Otto, by **counting in 10s**.
Write the number under the jar adding the extra bolts each time.

 10

3 Kora is helping Otto to tidy his workshop.
Each jar needs to have 10 bolts.

a Draw some more to make 10, or cross
some out if there are too many.
Write the number of bolts you have drawn or crossed out
under each jar.

b Count in 10s to find out how many bolts there are in total in **a**.

Fun Zone!

Have fun building terrific towers!
Build a tower with exactly 10 objects.
Now make more with different
objects.
Work out if this tower is as tall as the
last one.
Find 10 objects to build a tower as
tall as you are!

Congratulations!
You can now find and colour **Shape 6**
on the Monster Match page!

Monster Challenge 1

1

a Count how many **pairs** of balloons there are.

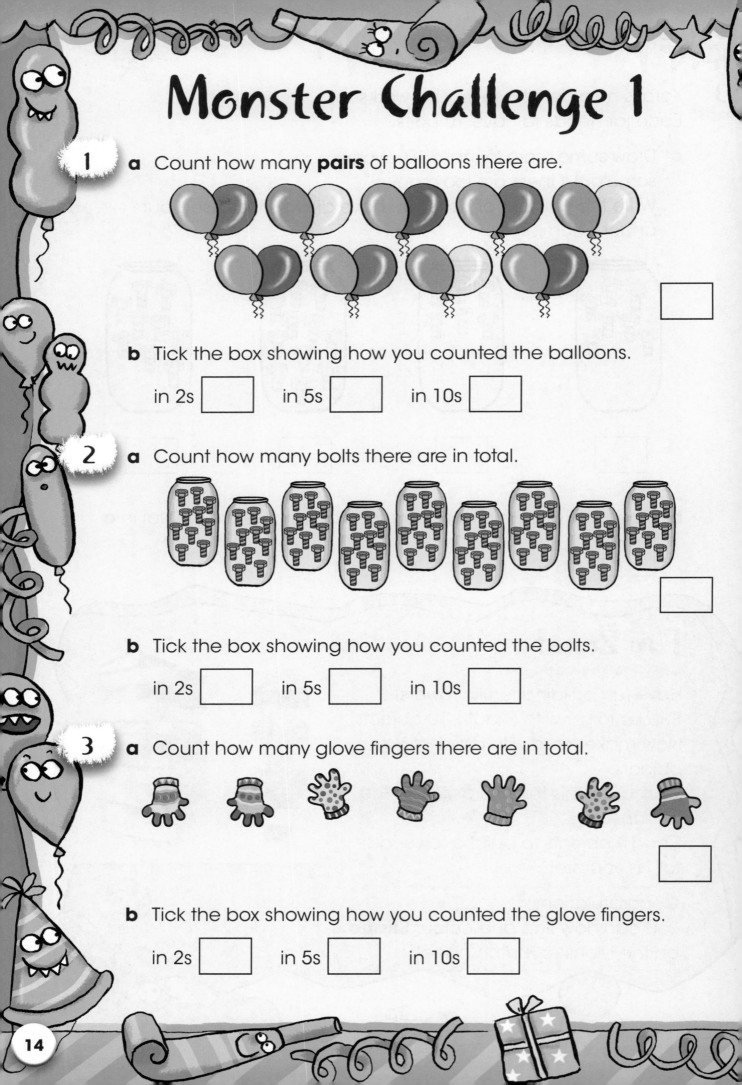

☐

b Tick the box showing how you counted the balloons.

in 2s ☐   in 5s ☐   in 10s ☐

2

a Count how many bolts there are in total.

☐

b Tick the box showing how you counted the bolts.

in 2s ☐   in 5s ☐   in 10s ☐

3

a Count how many glove fingers there are in total.

☐

b Tick the box showing how you counted the glove fingers.

in 2s ☐   in 5s ☐   in 10s ☐

4 Continue the number patterns.

a	2	4	6	8			
b	8	10	12				20
c	14				22	24	26
d	22	20	18	16			

5 Continue the number patterns.

a	25	30	35	40			
b	55	60	65				85
c	10				30	35	40
d	90	85	80	75			

6 Continue the number patterns.

a	40	50	60	70			
b	20	30	40				80
c	0				40	50	60
d	100	90	80	70			

7 Match each rectangle to the correct circle.

| 2 groups of 10 | 5 groups of 5 | 4 groups of 2 |

80   25   20   45   8   18

| 9 groups of 2 | 8 groups of 10 | 9 groups of 5 |

Monster Symbols

Grandpa keeps adding numbers and does not believe Kora when she says it would be much faster if he **multiplied**.

She challenges him to a counting race, and this is what happens.

Grandpa counts in 2s.

2 + 2 + 2 + 2 + 2 = 10

Kora counts the gloves.

She can see there are 5 piles of gloves, each with 2 gloves.

So, she multiplies 5 × 2 = 10.

Kora wins the counting race, because multiplying is faster than adding the same number lots of times.

Kora explains that the **multiplication symbol 'x'** means **'lots of'**.

1 Grandpa is still a bit confused. He needs to find the multiplication symbol, but has forgotten what it looks like. Help him by colouring in the squares which show the multiplication symbol.

×	÷	×	=	×
×	+	=	×	+
−	×	−	=	×
+	×	+	×	+
×	+	×	+	×

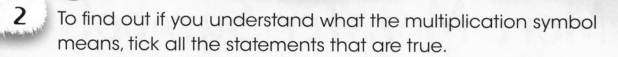

2 To find out if you understand what the multiplication symbol means, tick all the statements that are true.

Tick if true	Fact
	'Multiplication' means groups of the same number.
	'Multiplication' means to count backwards.
	'Multiplication' means your dinner is ready.
	'Multiplication' can be written with an 'x' symbol.

3 Practise writing the 'x' symbol.
Start at the red dot, join the dots and complete the line.

Fun Zone!

Colour the multiplication symbols to reveal the monster in the picture.

Well done! You can now find and colour **Shape 7** on the Monster Match page!

More Monster Symbols

Leckie has brought Grandpa some monster mice.
Grandpa wants to know how many ears there are in total.
Grandpa starts by counting how many mice there are.

He writes the answer in the first box.

| 2 | × | | = | |

Next, Grandpa counts how many ears
there are on 1 mouse.
He writes the answer in the next box.

| 2 | × | 2 | = | |

Grandpa knows that 2 lots of 2 = 4.
Grandpa puts the number 4 in the last box.

| 2 | × | 2 | = | 4 |

He knows that there are 4 ears in total.

1 Grandpa challenges you to a race!
Work out the answers by writing the number sentence under the
pictures as quickly as you can.

a Work out how many wheels there are on these bikes in total.

| | × | | = | |

b

☐ × ☐ = ☐

c

☐ × ☐ = ☐

Fun Zone!

Find the monster names in this word search.

Monsterific! You can now find and colour **Shape 8** on the Monster Match page!

Names can go up, down, across or diagonally.

GRANDPA
NANO
LECKIE
KORA
ZAK
LITMUS
MUM
GRAN

N	S	M	U	M	K	R	Q
S	A	T	K	G	O	I	S
S	A	N	I	G	R	A	N
U	B	Y	O	K	A	I	P
M	T	S	W	O	D	B	Z
T	G	R	A	N	D	P	A
I	L	C	Y	L	R	G	K
L	E	C	K	I	E	E	F

2 Times Table

Fizz is in a fluster with her **2 times table**!
She knows how to count in 2s but cannot multiply.
Kora has decided to help Fizz by teaching her how to 'jump' in 2s.

Kora uses a **number line** to help Fizz with her 2 times table.
A number line is very useful when multiplying.
We can 'jump' in 2s to count how many there are in total.

$2 \times 2 = 4$

1 Help Fizz find the answers to the following questions.

a $4 \times 2 = \boxed{}$ 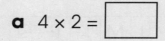

b $5 \times 2 = \boxed{}$ 0 2 4 6 8 10

c $3 \times 2 = \boxed{}$ 0 2 4 6 8 10

2 Now try these trickier questions.

a $7 \times 2 =$ ☐ 0 2 4 6 8 10 12 14 16 18 20

b $9 \times 2 =$ ☐ 0 2 4 6 8 10 12 14 16 18 20

3 Complete the 100 square by colouring in the 2 times table.
See if you can spot a pattern.

1	2	3	4	5	6	7	8	9	10
11	12	13	14	15	16	17	18	19	20
21	22	23	24	25	26	27	28	29	30
31	32	33	34	35	36	37	38	39	40
41	42	43	44	45	46	47	48	49	50
51	52	53	54	55	56	57	58	59	60
61	62	63	64	65	66	67	68	69	70
71	72	73	74	75	76	77	78	79	80
81	82	83	84	85	86	87	88	89	90
91	92	93	94	95	96	97	98	99	100

Fun Zone!

Join the dots in order
of the 2 times table
to reveal a picture.

Well done!
You can now find
and colour **Shape
9** on the Monster
Match page!

21

5 Times Table

Tizz is in trouble with her **5 times table**! Kora has decided to help Tizz by showing her how to use a number line to 'jump' in 5s.

A number line is very useful when multiplying.

We can 'jump' in 5s to count how many there are in total (counting the jumps will give you the answer).

$3 \times 5 = 15$

1 Use the number line to help you answer the questions below.

a $2 \times 5 =$ ☐ 0 5 10 15 20 25 30 35 40 45 50

b $4 \times 5 =$ ☐ 0 5 10 15 20 25 30 35 40 45 50

c $5 \times 5 =$ ☐ 0 5 10 15 20 25 30 35 40 45 50

2 Now use the number line to help you answer these questions.
Be careful with **e**, it is a tricky one!

a 6 × 5 = [　] **0** **5** **10** **15** **20** **25** **30** **35** **40** **45** **50**

b 9 × 5 = [　] **0** **5** **10** **15** **20** **25** **30** **35** **40** **45** **50**

c 7 × 5 = [　] **0** **5** **10** **15** **20** **25** **30** **35** **40** **45** **50**

d 8 × 5 = [　] **0** **5** **10** **15** **20** **25** **30** **35** **40** **45** **50**

e 0 × 5 = [　] **0** **5** **10** **15** **20** **25** **30** **35** **40** **45** **50**

Fun Zone!

Star jump challenge!
See how many star
jumps you can do in
1 minute and record
it on the table.
See if you can beat
your score tomorrow.

Day	Number of jumps

Fantastic!
You can now find and colour **Shape 10**
on the Monster Match page!

10 Times Table

Poggo is puzzled by the **10 times table** and does not know how to multiply by 10!
Kora has decided to help him by using a number line.
A number line is very useful when multiplying.
We can 'jump' in 10s to count how many there are in total (counting the jumps will give you the answer).

0 10 20 30 40 50 60 70 80 90 100

$4 \times 10 = 40$

1 Use the number lines to help Poggo solve the following questions.

a $3 \times 10 =$ ☐   0 10 20 30 40 50 60 70 80 90 100

b $2 \times 10 =$ ☐   0 10 20 30 40 50 60 70 80 90 100

c $5 \times 10 =$ ☐   0 10 20 30 40 50 60 70 80 90 100

2 Now try these trickier questions.

a $7 \times 10 =$ ☐   **0**   **10**   **20**   **30**   **40**   **50**   **60**   **70**   **80**   **90**   **100**

b $9 \times 10 =$ ☐   **0**   **10**   **20**   **30**   **40**   **50**   **60**   **70**   **80**   **90**   **100**

3 Complete the 100 square by colouring in the 10 times table.
See if you can spot a pattern.

1	2	3	4	5	6	7	8	9	10
11	12	13	14	15	16	17	18	19	20
21	22	23	24	25	26	27	28	29	30
31	32	33	34	35	36	37	38	39	40
41	42	43	44	45	46	47	48	49	50
51	52	53	54	55	56	57	58	59	60
61	62	63	64	65	66	67	68	69	70
71	72	73	74	75	76	77	78	79	80
81	82	83	84	85	86	87	88	89	90
91	92	93	94	95	96	97	98	99	100

Fun Zone!

Have fun making a monster collage!

Excellent!
You can now find and colour **Shape 11** on the Monster Match page!

Monster Collage

You will need a piece of white paper and some natural materials (e.g. leaves, twigs, bark, flowers, grass and stones).

Ask an adult to help when needed.

1 Collect some natural materials.

2 Place a white piece of paper on a flat surface.

3 Arrange your collection of natural materials into a monster face.

4 Move the items around to change the face.

Massive Monster Problems

Kora is helping the monsters to sort out these problems.
She knows that it is really important to look at all of the information and pick out the bits that are important.

Kora has 2 hands and 5 fingers on each hand.
How many fingers does she have **altogether**?

Kora knows that altogether means how many there are when working out 'lots of'.
She works out **2 lots of 5**.

$$2 \times 5 = 10$$

Kora has 10 fingers altogether.

1 Nano is going on holiday with his monster family.
Kora is working out how many bottles of milk Nano needs to take.
He drinks 2 bottles of milk per day and is going on holiday for 3 days.

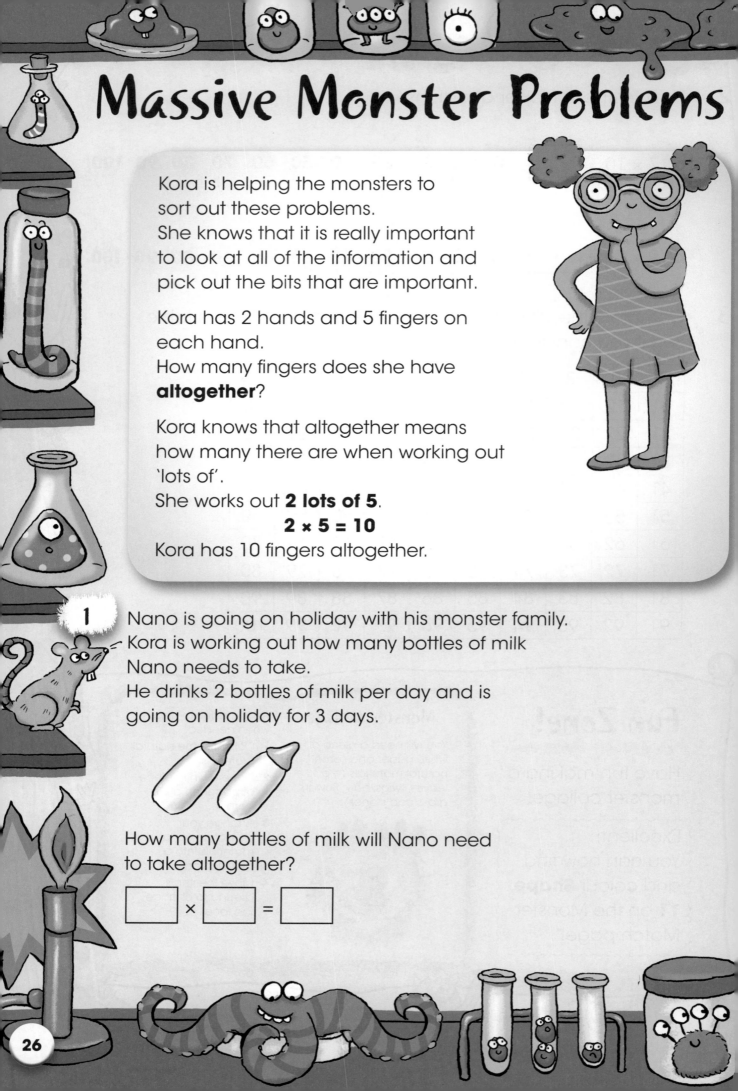

How many bottles of milk will Nano need to take altogether?

☐ × ☐ = ☐

2 Litmus is trying to make a new monster potion.
Here is a list of ingredients that he needs:
- 3 monster eyelashes
- 1 jar of monster slime
- 2 monster toe nails
- 5 **pairs** of monster eyeballs.

How many eyeballs will he need altogether?

	×		=	

3 Gran has seen lots of new mini-monsters on her travels.
She has found 10 new species and has seen 2 mini-monsters from each species.
How many mini-monsters has she seen altogether?

	×		=	

Fun Zone!

Put on your favourite music and make up your own monster dance. Think about how the monsters might move and the size of the monsters. Find an audience to watch your monster dance.

Very good! You can now find and colour **Shape 12** on the Monster Match page!

Monster Challenge 2

1 Draw a line to match the words to the symbols.

| times | add | take away | equals | multiply |

| + | = | × | – |

| subtract | plus | groups of | minus | makes |

2 Colour the jar with the correct answer.

a 6 × 2 =   15   10   12

b 3 × 5 =   20   15   8

c 9 × 10 =   10   90   18

d 7 × 2 =   14   40   24

e 8 × 5 =   35   45   40

f 4 × 10 =   35   40   400

3 Write the numbers coming out of the monster machines.

a

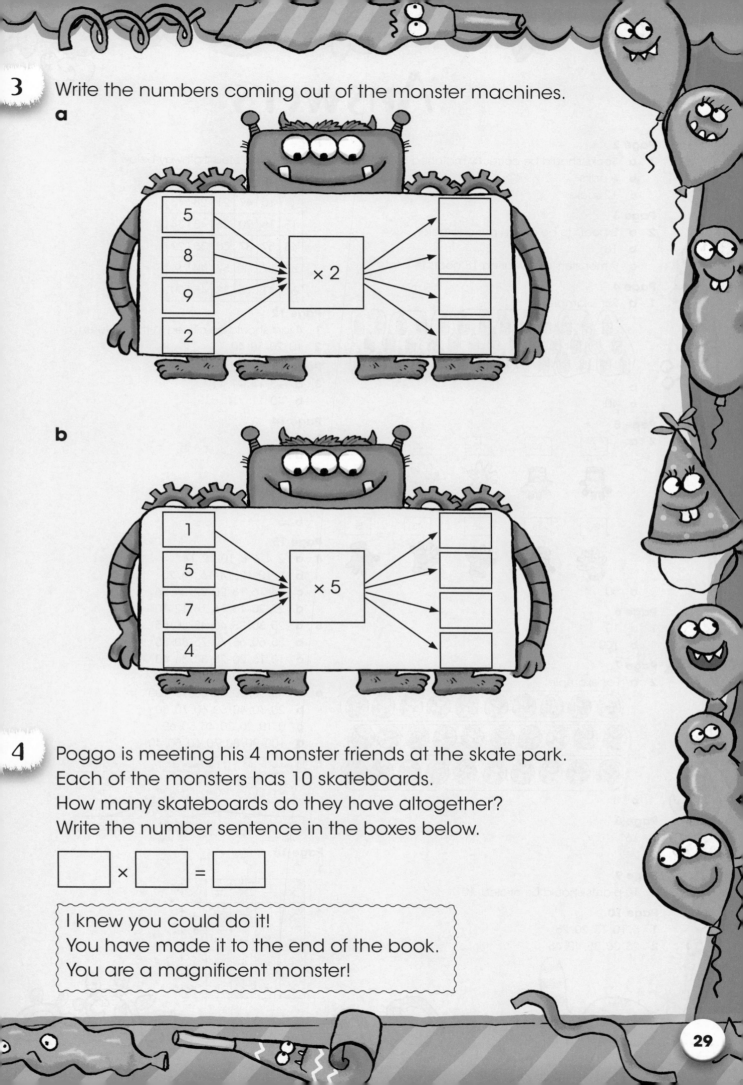

5
8
9
2

× 2

b

1
5
7
4

× 5

4 Poggo is meeting his 4 monster friends at the skate park.
Each of the monsters has 10 skateboards.
How many skateboards do they have altogether?
Write the number sentence in the boxes below.

[ ] × [ ] = [ ]

I knew you could do it!
You have made it to the end of the book.
You are a magnificent monster!

Answers

Page 2
1 a Socks should be correctly matched by pattern.
  b 6 pairs
  c 12 socks

Page 3
2 a 2 boots to be drawn per character.
  b 18
  c 9 monsters are wearing 18 boots in total.

Page 4
1 a For example:

  b 8
  c 40

Page 5
2 a

5	10	15	20	25

30	35	40	45	50

  b 50

Page 6
1 a 10
  b 100

Page 7
2 a For example:

  b 3

Page 8
1 16
2 24

Page 9
3 10 plants should be circled; 10

Page 10
1 5, 10, 15, 20, 25
2 25, 30, 35, 40, 45

Page 11
3 See completed pathway below.

0	8	12	34	18	4
5	10	47	21	28	73
13	15	20	25	43	34
48	52	37	30	35	22
33	87	1	57	40	9
67	41	16	38	45	50

Page 12
1 4 jars should be circled in the picture.
2 10, 20, 30, 40

Page 13
3 a +3, +4, −1, +1
  b 40

Page 14
1 a 9
  b 2s
2 a 90
  b 10s
3 a 35
  b 5s

Page 15
4 a 2, 4, 6, 8, 10, 12, 14
  b 8, 10, 12, 14, 16, 18, 20
  c 14, 16, 18, 20, 22, 24, 26
  d 22, 20, 18, 16, 14, 12, 10
5 a 25, 30, 35, 40, 45, 50, 55
  b 55, 60, 65, 70, 75, 80, 85
  c 10, 15, 20, 25, 30, 35, 40
  d 90, 85, 80, 75, 70, 65, 60
6 a 40, 50, 60, 70, 80, 90, 100
  b 20, 30, 40, 50, 60, 70, 80
  c 0, 10, 20, 30, 40, 50, 60
  d 100, 90, 80, 70, 60, 50, 40
7

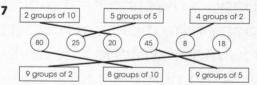

Page 16
1

×	÷	×	=	×
×	+	=	×	+
−	×	−	=	×
+	×	+	×	+
×	+	×	+	×

2

Tick if true	Fact
✔	'Multiplication' means groups of the same number.
	'Multiplication' means to count backwards.
	'Multiplication' means your dinner is ready.
✔	'Multiplication' can be written with an 'x' symbol.

3 Child to join the dots and complete the line.

Fun Zone

Page 18
1 a $4 \times 2 = 8$

Page 19
  b $3 \times 2 = 6$ **c** $6 \times 2 = 12$

Fun Zone

N	S	M	U	M	K	R	Q
S	A	T	K	G	O	I	S
S	A	N	I	G	R	A	N
U	B	Y	O	K	A	I	P
M	T	S	W	O	D	B	Z
T	G	R	A	N	D	P	A
I	L	C	Y	L	R	G	K
L	E	C	K	I	E	E	F

Page 20
1 a $4 \times 2 = 8$ **b** $5 \times 2 = 10$ **c** $3 \times 2 = 6$

Page 21
2 a $7 \times 2 = 14$ **b** $9 \times 2 = 18$
3

1	2	3	4	5	6	7	8	9	10
11	12	13	14	15	16	17	18	19	20
21	22	23	24	25	26	27	28	29	30
31	32	33	34	35	36	37	38	39	40
41	42	43	44	45	46	47	48	49	50
51	52	53	54	55	56	57	58	59	60
61	62	63	64	65	66	67	68	69	70
71	72	73	74	75	76	77	78	79	80
81	82	83	84	85	86	87	88	89	90
91	92	93	94	95	96	97	98	99	100

Fun Zone

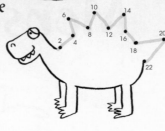

Page 22
1 a $2 \times 5 = 10$ **b** $4 \times 5 = 20$ **c** $5 \times 5 = 25$

Page 23
2 a $6 \times 5 = 30$ **c** $7 \times 5 = 35$ **e** $0 \times 5 = 0$
  b $9 \times 5 = 45$ **d** $8 \times 5 = 40$

Page 24
1 a $3 \times 10 = 30$ **b** $2 \times 10 = 20$ **c** $5 \times 10 = 50$

Page 25
2 a $7 \times 10 = 70$ **b** $9 \times 10 = 90$
3

1	2	3	4	5	6	7	8	9	10
11	12	13	14	15	16	17	18	19	20
21	22	23	24	25	26	27	28	29	30
31	32	33	34	35	36	37	38	39	40
41	42	43	44	45	46	47	48	49	50
51	52	53	54	55	56	57	58	59	60
61	62	63	64	65	66	67	68	69	70
71	72	73	74	75	76	77	78	79	80
81	82	83	84	85	86	87	88	89	90
91	92	93	94	95	96	97	98	99	100

Page 26
1 $3 \times 2 = 6$

Page 27
2 $5 \times 2 = 10$
3 $10 \times 2 = 20$

Page 28
1
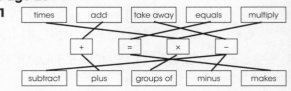

2 a $6 \times 2 = 12$ **d** $7 \times 2 = 14$
  b $3 \times 5 = 15$ **e** $8 \times 5 = 40$
  c $9 \times 10 = 90$ **f** $4 \times 10 = 40$

Page 29
3 a $5 \times 2 = 10$; $8 \times 2 = 16$; $9 \times 2 = 18$; $2 \times 2 = 4$
  b $1 \times 5 = 5$; $5 \times 5 = 25$; $7 \times 5 = 35$; $4 \times 5 = 20$
4 $4 \times 10 = 40$

Monster Match

Each time you complete a topic in this book, you will be awarded a shape number.

Find and colour the shapes in the picture of Dad that match the numbers you have been given.

As you work through the book you will gradually see Dad come to life!